Tiger Sharks

Gina Cline   Gee Johnson

This is a shark.

This is a tiger shark. A tiger shark has stripes like a tiger.

3

 **4** The tiger shark lives in the ocean.
The tiger shark looks like the ocean.

The tiger shark looks gray from above.

5

6

When you're under a tiger shark, it looks white.

Tiger sharks swim fast.

 8

They have fins like this.

They have tails like this.

Tiger sharks have many teeth.

They have good noses.

Tiger sharks eat stingrays.

12

They eat turtles.

13

They eat seals and birds.

They can eat people.

They will eat all of these, too.

16

Tiger sharks like to eat lots!

18

This is a baby shark.

The mom shark has live babies.

20

She can have up to 80 babies in one day!

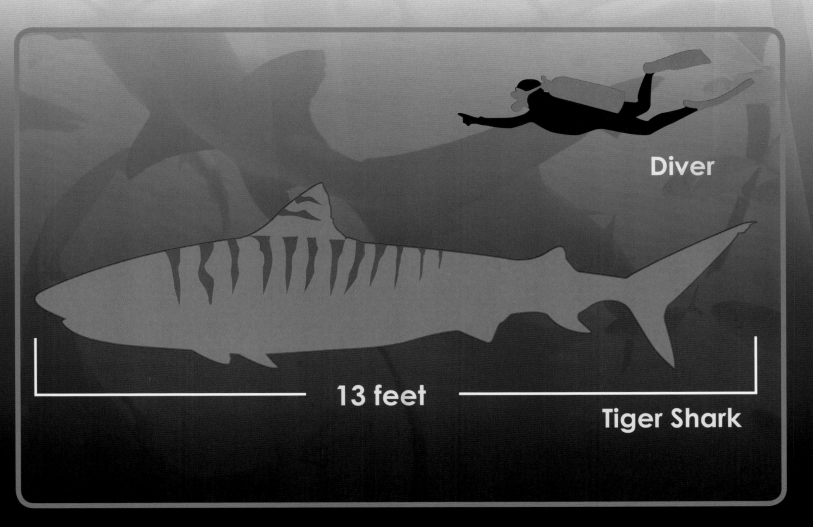

Diver

13 feet

Tiger Shark

The tiger shark can be this big.

22

Tiger sharks do not live in a family.
Big sharks will eat the baby sharks.

Swim, baby shark!

23

Power Words

How many can you read?

a	eat	look	they
above	family	lots	this
all	from	many	to
and	good	mom	too
baby	has	not	under
be	have	of	up
big	in	one	when
can	is	she	white
day	like	the	will
do	live	these	you're

24